The Problem
of Pleasure

Why Good Things Happen to Bad People

by

Dr. John H. Gerstner

Soli Deo Gloria Publications
. . . *for instruction in righteousness* . . .

Soli Deo Gloria Publications
A division of Soli Deo Gloria Ministries, Inc.
P. O. Box 451, Morgan PA 15064
(412) 221-1901/FAX 221-1902
www.SDGbooks.com

*

*

ISBN 1-57358-138-0

*

Library of Congress Cataloging-in-Publication Data

Gerstner, John H. (John Henry), 1914-1996.
    The Problem of Pleasure: why good things
happen to bad people/by John H. Gerstner.
        p. cm.
ISBN 1-57358-138-0 (booklet: alk.paper)
1. Pleasure—Religious aspects—Christianity.
I. Title.
BV4597.59 G47 2002
231.7—dc21
                                        2001007738

Contents

Just about everybody thinks there is a problem of pain. Even philosophers assume that the most formidable theoretical problem is that of suffering. The most grievous question, however, is why pain constitutes a problem, for the real problem lies elsewhere. It may trouble you as a reader to learn of someone who thinks pain is not a problem. You have thought it obvious not only that there is pain, but also that pain in a world created by a good God is indeed a problem. Since no one in this world escapes adversity altogether, no one doubts that there is pain in the world. Some of this pain is excruciating. In fact, some people face more distress than comfort. Apart from Christian Scientists, no one we know denies that pain hurts.

The Non-Problem of Pain

Pain and suffering raise a dilemma. Philosophers commonly argue: "If God is good, then He is not all-powerful; and if He is all-powerful, then He is not good." Suffering, they insist, is not compatible with an omnipotent, benevolent deity. If God were both good and omnipotent, He would never allow suffering. Since misery and suffering do occur, He is either not good or He is not all-powerful.

A few theologians say that God is omnipotent though not good. They think of Him as being beyond good and evil and indifferent to finite happenings, or as having created the world in such a way that pain simply comes about when people violate the laws of the created universe. God, somewhat abstracted from it all, could not care less about the relentlessness of created nature. It is a kind of self-correcting universe; people have to pay the price of pain when they tinker with it. God Himself does not tinker with it, and thus there are no miracles.

The Indian god, Bhagwan, exemplifies this thought. A picture on the temple wall showed this deity bending over the prone figure of a human being and pulling out the victim's entrails. One tourist asked the meaning of the painting and was told that it "shows Bhagwan's power." Apparently Bhagwan, though not good, was irresistible and did not hesitate to show his strength by torturing those less powerful than he.

The more common philosophical solution, however, is to give up not the goodness of God, but rather His omnipotence. God is indeed good, but suffering proves that He simply is not able to achieve universal happiness. He would like to, and if He were able He would. Since He does not, He is not able. When God is put in the dock, He is cleared of any guilt of ill will. He is simply less powerful than He is benevolent.

The idea of a finite God has had a long history from Plato to Edgar Sheffield Brightman. God may be infinite in His goodness, but He is finite in other qualities, especially power. He is a limited deity as far as His ability to execute His desires is concerned. The result is the tragic story of human misery. William James, one of the most noted preachers of the finite God, goes even further than that. In one of his most noted comments, he remarked that there is a problem of suffering as long as one cockroach pines in unrequited love. I myself will have to admit that my faith was challenged when in a museum many years ago I saw an artificial representation of a hawk pulling apart a tiny bird. "Nature red in tooth and claw" nearly overpowered my belief in an omnipotently good deity. We sympathize with William James's suffering cockroach, and agree with him that, if there is a problem of pain at all, it is not restricted to human beings. Wherever there is any anguish, there is the problem of pain.

We need not further illustrate what is meant by the problem of pain. What probably troubles the reader is having been told that there is *no* problem of pain—especially since the writer is not a Christian Scientist, but actually admits that pain hurts. How could anyone imagine that pain raises no problem in a universe in which an omnipotently benevolent deity reigns supreme?

The answer to that so-called problem of pain is sin. As long as there is sin, there can be no problem of pain. A good God, if He is omnipotent, would have to make the sinner suffer.

A dilemma would exist only if there were no suffering in a sinful world. Then we would have to say there cannot be a true God. Were there no adversity in a sinful world, God either would not be good or would not be omnipotent. Either He would be unconcerned about sin's being unpunished, and therefore not good, or He would be unable to punish sin, and therefore not omnipotent. That would be a real problem in our world, where sin obviously abounds.

What could you possibly expect in a sinful world but suffering? If there were no suffering, then you would have an absolutely unanswerable problem: How could God be all-powerful and all-good and allow sin to go unpunished?

The Real Problem Is Pleasure

Troubled by the non-problem of pain, most people do not feel the real problem. The real difficulty is the problem of pleasure. While in a sinful world, pain is to be expected, and pleasure is not to be expected. We should be constantly amazed at the presence of pleasure in a world such as ours.

It is easy to understand why this confusion has come about. Pain is a painful subject. Pleasure is a pleasurable subject. People do not like pain. They do like pleasure. And people associate problems with what they do not like. Because they do not like pain, they call it a problem.

The fact is that pain is no problem, whereas pleasure is an excruciating problem; and if one ever begins to think about that it can become intolerable. How could there be pleasure in a sinful world? People do not like thinking about pleasure in such a light because then they must admit their own sinfulness.

On the other hand, there is a kind of relief from pain in viewing it as an undeserved problem. We imply that the blame for our affliction lies elsewhere. That soothes our pain a little by assuring us that we do not deserve such misery. But if pain is a non-problem, it is so because we deserve punishment. Calling it a "non-problem" is a frank admission that we are sinners and, therefore, may not complain about it.

So when we call pain a problem, we claim we do not deserve it. We are even prepared to scuttle God to maintain our own innocence. We will say that God is not able to do what He would like, or He would never permit persons such as ourselves to suffer. That puffs up our egos and soothes our griefs at the same time. "How could God do this to *me*?" is at once an admission of pain and a soporific for it. It reduces our personal grief by eradicating the deity. Drastic medicine, indeed, that only a human ego, run wild, could possibly imagine.

Why Pain Is Not the Problem

So that there are no doubts that pain is a non-problem, three points may be made: first, there is sin; second, sin requires suffering; and, third, therefore, suffering is not a problem, not even eternal suffering, which is the ultimate form of it.

The Fact of Sin

First, then, the easy part, that there is sin in the world. Karl Menninger wrote a book entitled, *Whatever Happened to Sin?* Well, as the doctor admits, sin is still here. It is just that people do not so willingly acknowledge that fact. A spade is no longer called a spade, but some euphemism. The little boy says to his mother, "Why is it that whenever I do anything bad, it's because I'm a bad boy; but whenever you do anything bad, it's because you're nervous?" It is nerves rather than sin. It is our glands rather than sin. It is what we eat, the environment, our biorhythm, rather than sin. In fact, it is anything but sin. Sin denies that it is sin.

The ultimate form of any vice is to deny that it is a vice, and rather to rejoice in it. That is denial with a vengeance, actually making a virtue of it. John Barrymore used to say that he did not like to be obscene and not heard. His obscenity, for him, was a virtue that deserved to be displayed and admired; he wanted praise for it. Whether or not we have become hardened so as to make sin a virtue, we certainly have made sin sinless.

No one would ever read the Bible and get the impression that God is in His Heaven and all's well with the world. Sin started with the first man, according to the Bible. In Adam all sinned. Sin came into the world through the transgression of one man. But many view the Bible as antiquated and obsolete. People who deny sin deny what I am saying right now as I affirm sin. They will say, "Nonsense." When they realize that I have a Ph.D. from Harvard, they will say, "That is utterly inexcusable for a person such as he not to know that sin is a mere name, and not a real entity at all." As a matter of fact, they could get up quite a head of steam and even tell me: "You *ought* to know better." When a person says to me, "You ought to know better," he means that I am sinning by saying what I do. I am doing what is wrong, and I am inexcusable because I should know better. That is essentially what we mean by sin, violating the moral law. One ought to act according to his understanding of truth. These persons feel that I should understand the truth that there is no such thing as sin. Consequently, by affirming sin, I am telling a falsehood, which I should not do. They blame me for this and reprimand me for this wrongdoing. They say to me that I am not the type of person I ought to be. That is a rebuke as well as a definition. It is showing what sin means, and that I am a sinner, and that I deserve the verbal punishment (at least) that they give me by so labeling me.

So while they deny sin, they affirm sin. If they really did not believe that there is such a thing as sin, they would not, in effect, call me a sinner. But if they do call me a sinner, by that word or by a euphemism, then they show that they do not believe that sin is obsolete. So they find themselves in a predicament of wanting to deny sin, but unable to do so without affirming it. Sin is not only not obsolete, it is not obsolescent; and, indeed, it never can become obsolete while this world remains as it is. God's Word has not fallen too far behind the avalanche of contemporary literature. We may tell Dr. Menninger that the only thing that has happened to sin is that people now, rather than affirming it by affirming it, prefer to affirm it by denying it.

Those who affirm sin by denying it are doubly sinners. When they call me a sinner because I ought to know better than to affirm sin, they are themselves affirming sin. Though sinning itself is bad enough, denying sin is an additional sin, so that those who deny sin are actually double sinners. In a certain sense, they argue more strenuously for sin than we traditionalists do. And they have more opportunity for sinning than we do because denying that sin exists is not a possibility for those who believe the Bible.

So, then, there is sin. Not only does the Word of God say so, but, what is far more impressive to our culture, twentieth-century intellectuals say so with a vengeance.

Sin Requires Punishment

Second, sin deserves punishment. Dr. Karl Menninger asked, "Whatever happened to sin?" He should write another book entitled, *Whatever Happened to Punishment?* In the opinion of many, not only does crime not deserve punishment, but punishment is the crime. Menninger himself wrote *The Crime of Punishment.* But when a person says that crime does not deserve punishment, he is taking the heinousness out of the criminal act. He thinks that crime does not spring from the actor, but from some external circumstance—his ghetto background or his privileged status with its irresponsibilities. "It's not your son's fault," said the maid to Reinhold Niebuhr. The son of the famous theologian had been in a neighborhood brawl and was somewhat worse for wear when the maid interceded with the father, who was about to finish what the neighborhood kids had started. "It is not your son's fault—it is the company he keeps." Neibuhr's response to the maid's entreaty was, "It is not the company he keeps; it is his own little black heart." The maid championed the thesis that there is no crime except punishment, whereas Niebuhr, in this case, expressed the sentiment that there is crime, and it does deserve punishment.

I think we would all agree that crime deserves punishment. Those who say that it does not say so quite consistently, because they argue that it is *not* crime. We agree that where there is no crime, there needs be no punishment. The question is a matter of fact rather than value judgment.

Is there such a thing as crime? We have already answered that question. If there is such a thing as sin, there is such a thing as crime, a specific form of sin. And if we all agree that there is such a thing as crime, or sin, then it deserves punishment. When I am told, "You *ought* to know better," I am not only being informed, I am being rebuked. That indictment amounts to a punishment for my sin of saying there is such a thing as sin. So those who say such things prove both points—that there is sin, and that sin ought to be punished. If they rebuke me verbally, and I do not mend my ways, the question could well come up whether I ought to receive some other form of punishment. They are convinced of one thing: I ought to be punished in the most effective way.

Most intellectuals are opposed to corporal punishment because they do not think it is effective, and they argue against capital punishment, that it does not deter crime. Futile punishment ought not to be administered. Capital punishment, since these people think it is futile, is resisted not because it is punishment, but because it is not punishment, that is, it is ineffective. They want crime deterred, but by an effective form of punishment. It seems, no matter how people express it, they must acknowledge that there is sin, and that sin deserves to be punished. The only differences among us have to do with the names we give to sin and the shape punishment should take.

Consider our opinion about capital punishment with respect to the killing of police officers. Why would that question ever come up? If punishment is a crime, then of course the killing of a policeman should not be punished either. When we make distinctions between killing civilians and killing policemen, we show that certain kinds of crime, at least, deserve punishment. But no one is saying that crimes do not deserve punishment. The question is *what* crimes do, and what punishment is effective. Apparently, some believe that though capital punishment is not effective with civilians when civilians are the victims, it may be effective and necessary when policemen are the victims. There seems to be a general impression that capital punishment in the case of murderers of police is a deterrent and therefore ought to be administered.

One form of capital punishment everybody seems to approve: killing an attacker in self-defense. That is, most people will defend saving one's own life, even if it requires taking the life of the would-be killer. There is a great division of opinion among us at the present time whether killers, *after* they have killed, should be killed. But there is virtually no difference of opinion that killers, *before* they are successful in killing, should be killed, if that is the only way that they can be stopped.

Punishment Requires Pain

Third, suffering is necessary. If there is such a thing as sin, and sin deserves to be punished, then the punishment must be administered, and punishment that does not hurt is not punishment. We may insist that the punishment is ameliorative or helpful, ultimately, but nobody is drawing up a proposition that punishment is not painful. It is self-evident that if punishment is not painful, it is not punishment. The only point of punishment is the administration of pain. The person who does sin, who commits a crime, deserves to be punished; he deserves to suffer. One hopes that suffering will cure him of his sinfulness. At least, it will correct his behavior. He will be "scared straight" in behavior, if not softened in spirit.

In human affairs, pain is no problem. Even in *our* conduct, if we did not administer pain under certain circumstances, that would be a problem. It would, we think, be wrong.

Our main problem is that so much crime goes unpunished. Murderers—proven, demonstrated murderers—serve an average of about eight years in prison for killing another human being in cold blood. But most murderers are not caught at all and not punished at all. Our thinking is loose and our laws are not what they ought to be. Even judging our performance according to our own inadequate standards, we are far short of the mark. We recognize that our crime lies in nonpunishment rather than in punishment, though occasionally the punishment itself is the crime when it is excessive or when it is punishment of the wrong person. Fundamentally, our own culture in our own estimate falls under our own condemnation of not fitting the punishment to the crime, even approximately.

But when we consider God, we realize that He would see sin perfectly because sin, in the last analysis, is against Him. He is the author of the moral law by which we are constrained. "Where there is no law there is no sin." Furthermore, if even we can see that sin should be punished, He would see with perfect and infinite vision that sin should be punished. Most important of all, if we punish crime (very, very imperfectly), He will punish it perfectly, precisely because He is both good and omnipotent. Therefore, we have no problem with pain inflicted by God, if it can be shown that the person suffering it deserves it, and that it is in the measure which he deserves. These two characteristics we assume, of course, would describe a divine act of punishment or infliction of pain.

Because every man is a sinner, every man deserves the wrath of God. Manifestly, he is not getting anything that approximates, much less exceeds, the wrath of God in this world. Manifestly, "he" is all of us, since we all are sinners. We deserve to suffer because, without exception, we are sinners; and in fact, we all deserve far more than we receive.

If someone says, "Look, I read in the paper just today about some gangsters exchanging bullets and an *innocent* bystander being killed. The innocent bystander was killed. You don't call that divine justice, do you? Maybe the gangsters deserved to kill each other and be killed, but the innocent bystander, by definition, didn't deserve to be killed, did he?"

"You're right," we reply. "Innocent people don't deserve to be killed. And the man was innocent of any particular crime that concerned these two who were exchanging bullets." Those two men would agree that he didn't deserve to die. It was the other criminal, the first criminal will insist, who deserved to die. He will even say, "I didn't mean to kill that bystander. He should have watched himself and stayed out of the fire. Too bad. But the other guy I was trying to shoot deserved to be killed. I'm glad I got him. I'm sorry about this innocent bystander."

Yes, the man was innocent as far *as their quarrel was concerned*, but was he an innocent bystander in the sight of God? Obviously not, if what we have already said is true. He was a sinner under the wrath of God who had not begun to receive the full punishment he deserved. So, as far as God was concerned, he deserved that bullet. As far as God was concerned, he was not an innocent bystander. As far as God was concerned, he was a criminal too, who was receiving a deserved bullet which the *gangster* had no right to shoot, but which *God* had every right to allow to be shot. This bystander was innocent before the man who shot him, but guilty before the God who ordained permissively that he be shot.

Do people really deserve to suffer at God's hand, and are

they fairly punished? It is clear that they deserve to be punished because they are sinners, and that they have been fairly, not excessively, punished because they are sinners against God, against an infinite God.

Why Do the "Righteous" Suffer?

Again, a protest arises: "What about the suffering of the righteous? Is the Bible not full of the complaints of godly people who are afflicted while the wicked flourish as a green bay tree? Is the Bible not against you in saying that some righteous do suffer and some sinners do not suffer?"

Take, first, the charge that the wicked prosper rather than suffer. That is the lament of the godly at times. The Bible grants that many wicked persons continue to live and flourish in this world, much to the dismay of the righteous. But the Bible does not teach that the wicked do not suffer. It does teach that they suffer, but not as much as they deserve to suffer. In many instances, they do not endure as much physical suffering as the saints, who are often martyred. But the Bible does not present the wicked as not being punished. It simply says they do not receive their full punishment in this world. God has a better way of administering justice than that.

Likewise, the godly do suffer and complain about it at times. But the Bible teaches plainly that their suffering, even after their conversion and reconciliation to God, is not punishment any longer, but chastening. It is not the punishment of a God who is angry with them, but the chastening of a God who is reconciled to them. Whom God loves, the Scripture says, He chastens. He makes all things, including pain, "work together for good for them that love God, and are called according to His purpose." This should be the consolation and strength of saints. They are far from perfect, so they lapse into complaining at times. They forget the divine purpose, momentarily, under the smarting of their grief. But the Bible does not say that the righteous

suffer, any more than it says that the unrighteous do not
suffer. The unrighteous suffer, but not as much as they deserve to or ultimately will suffer; and the righteous
painfully suffer, but they do not suffer pain. That affliction
is actually a blessing in disguise. At times, they can see
through the disguise. At other times, the pain hurts so
much that they cannot, through their tears, see the disguise. Momentarily they lament the heavy hand of God
upon them, but when they are thinking in their most
saintly character, they praise God. His rod and staff comfort
them.

Job, for example, was permitted some awesome catas-
trophes for the good of his soul. It did indeed do his soul,
and ultimately his body, great good, as we know from that
famous book of the Old Testament. Job was like a modern
saint who suffered so dreadfully, but said that he did not
"have a pain to spare." When pain is present it is difficult to
bear; but when a Christian, even in anguish, realizes that
this is the heavy hand of a loving God upon him, he blesses
God in his suffering and for his suffering, which he knows
is for his own good and for his everlasting blessedness.

So, in spite of all the intellectual agonizing about the
problem of pain, the only problem is explaining why pain
is a *problem*. In a sinful world pain is axiomatic. No one
should ever have been surprised about its presence. It
would have been a problem only if it did not exist. If this is
the imperial problem of philosophers and theologians, this
emperor has no clothes.

Only as an emotional and physical "problem" is pain
real, and, as such, the only real problem is that pain hurts.
That is easy to understand, but insuperably difficult to endure. So mankind should expend its intellectual energies not
on a non-problem of pain, but on how to escape it. "What
must I do to be saved?"

Absence of Pain Would Be a Real Problem
If there were no pain in this world, there would be a real

problem. But, since there is pain, there is no dilemma because we know that this sinful world deserves precisely that. The present pain is not sufficient to our crimes, so that we can ask, Why so little pain? Why so much pleasure? Why *any* pleasure?

This is the real difficulty. Why is there any pleasure in this world? There is no problem of pain, but there is an omnipresent problem of pleasure. If God was in His heaven, and all were well with the world, then we would know that this world is indeed a paradise. Since, though God is in heaven, all is not well in the world, the question is, Why so little punishment? God is a being of infinite glory. Sin against Him is sin of infinite enormity. We say that sin is sin. But there is another sense in which sin is not sin. One sin is vastly different from another sin. It has the same nature, to be sure, but the different degree of it eclipses what it has in common.

For example, two boys get into a scrap, and one of them gets beaten up more than the other. Suppose he deserved it, had done something which required a bit of thrashing. Nobody's eyebrows are raised much as long as there has been no permanent damage. Just two kids fighting it out over some grievance.

Suppose the same kid, however, beat up his mother as much as he beat up his friend. Would anyone ever say that is the same sin? The beating is the same, but the offense is vastly greater. Why? Because the boys are peers; they are more or less equal to one another. But in their filial relationships, the mother is nearer than the boy's peers. She is also much more significant than her son as the source and preservation of his being. He has a divine command to honor and obey her. He owes everything to her, including life itself. For him to be disobedient to her would be a very great offense, but actually to beat her would be an unspeakable one because she is his mother. We would say that if he only spoke back disrespectfully to his mother, without even touching her, that offense would be greater than giving his neighbor a severe thrashing.

We see this principle generally in human affairs. Even our soft culture (where capital punishment is considered the crime) recognizes a difference between killing a policeman and killing a civilian. It is the same murder, to be sure, but to murder a person risking his life to prevent murder is considered more iniquitous than to murder the person, for example, who may have provoked it. Both are just as dead, but we recognize the difference between the two murders.

Again, a man kills a peer; that is terrible. But if he attacks and kills a defenseless old lady who has befriended him all his life, does anyone say that is the same crime? It is the same murder. Both persons are equally dead. But more is owed to one than to the other. Consequently, a violation of that obligation makes one crime more heinous than the other.

There is no comparison at all between God and any of His creatures. In fact, all our sins against our fellowman are ultimately sins only because God has forbidden these deeds. "Against Thee and Thee only have I sinned," cried David, after committing adultery and murder. In sexually contaminating Bathsheba, and politically executing her innocent husband, David was guilty of two capital crimes. Each one of these, however, was a crime in any degree only because it was a violation of the divine commandment. "Against Thee and Thee only have I sinned." In adultery and murder, lying and theft, and any other particular sin, we have sinned "against Thee and Thee only." Instead of reducing the severity of these crimes because they are directed against one person only, it aggravates them, because that one person is infinitely more valuable than all the creatures combined. And if we recognize degrees of heinousness between a crime against one human being and another, we can see that the difference between a crime against a human and against the divine Being is infinite, and requires an infinitely more severe punishment.

The Problem: Why So Little Pain?

This is a sinful world, and sin is ultimately against its Creator, God. That sin is infinitely heinous and deserving of infinite punishment. All that mankind has suffered, in all of the ages at the hands of an angry God whose holiness has been obscured and whose justice has been violated, does not add up to one offense against the deity.

In this light, we see the problem of pleasure. Manifestly, as sinners against an infinitely glorious God, we deserve an immediate and infinite, condign, irremediable punishment from His holy, powerful hands. Nothing that we have ever received, that anyone has ever received, in all this world, has even approximated an adequate punishment for the crimes we commit in any one moment. How, therefore, do we continue to live? Why are we not plunged into eternal torment now, immediately?

What irony that sinners consider the greatest problem they face in this world to be the problem of pain. The ultimate insult against God is that man thinks he has a problem of pain. Man, who deserves to be plunged into hell at this moment, and is indescribably fortunate that he is breathing normally, complains about unhappiness. Instead of falling on his knees in the profoundest possible gratitude that God holds back His wrath and infinite fury, the sinner shakes his fist in heaven's face and complains against what he calls "pain." When he receives his due, he will look back on his present condition as paradisaical. What he now calls misery, he will then consider exquisite pleasure. The most severe torment anyone has ever known in this life will seem like heaven in comparison with one moment of the full fury of the divine Being.

The most foolish thing a human being ever says is that "the only hell there is in this world." The truth of the matter is that, for that person, the only *heaven* there is is in this world. When he goes to hell for his unbelief, he will realize that the only heaven he ever knew was in this world, which he called "hell." How he will then cry out for a moment of what he now calls "hell!"

Anyone who is aware of the existence of God and of sin cannot help but wonder about the problem of pleasure. "How long, O Lord, how long?" the saints cry out. They are especially aware of the predicament when they see the wicked flourish as the green bay tree. But the thoughtful saint, when he sees the wicked existing in the most miserable circumstances (as far as possible from flourishing as the green bay tree), wonders how long the Lord will put up with such iniquity and so little punishment. Time and again the psalmist cries to God as if he thinks God were sleeping. God punishes so little the evil which deserves so much that the psalmist, in his moments of despair, concludes that God must be sleeping. He would shake Him and wake Him up so that God would show how angry He is against the wicked. The Scripture says that God is "angry with the wicked every day." The saint knows that, but wonders why, if God is angry, infinitely angry with the wicked every day, He shows so little of His wrath.

The wicked, in turn, draw a false consolation from their relative comfort. When they flourish, they suppose that "the Man upstairs" is pleased with them, that He is blind to their faults, that they are able to pull the wool over His eyes as they do over their business associates and others who are their victims. Some of them get away, literally with murder. Nothing happens to them. The "Lucky Lucianos," as they are called, come and go. They kill, they rape, they steal, they lie, they threaten. So far from being punished for it, they seem to be blessed by it. Honesty pays, but it is not obvious in their cases. Crime is not supposed to pay, but it certainly seems as if it is very lucrative, especially in an age such as ours when more of the sympathy is for the victimizer than for his victims.

The Bible indicates that God hates the wicked. He is not only angry with them, He actually hates them. "Thou dost hate all who do iniquity" (Psalm 5:5). "The one who loves violence His soul hates" (Psalm 11:5). He hates liars and covenant breakers. He hates persons such as Esau, who prefer their mess of pottage to their spiritual birthright.

Yet, as the Lord says, He makes the sun to shine and the rain to fall on the unjust and the wicked as well as on the godly. And His followers are required to act accordingly. Christ commands us to love our enemies, and uses as His model the fact that God from heaven showers His blessings on the wicked. We see that God actually hates and is infinitely angry with persons upon whom He pours great blessings. We are not allowed to hate persons, but are commanded to love them. We cannot, of course, be pleased with persons who hate God and hate us, but we can behave lovingly toward them and pray for them. In so doing, we follow the model of God.

All of this only accentuates our problem—the problem of pleasure. We observe in life that mankind generally prospers. There is much sickness, suffering, loneliness, emptiness, and sorrow, to be sure; but it is not in any proportion to the blessing most people receive. One would hardly believe that God really hates the wicked and is infinitely angry with them, judging from the way He behaves toward them. It perplexes the godly and is misinterpreted by the wicked themselves, as if it were a token of divine permission at least, and favor at most. So the Bible, instead of relieving the problem at this point, seems to aggravate it. It reveals God as knowingly participating in this crime; that is, He is visiting untold blessings upon people whom He actually hates. Coupled with His anger, which is unceasing toward the wicked, He gives them many tokens of forbearance and love.

Why Does God Permit Pleasure?

What is the solution to the problem of pleasure? Suppose there was no revelation from God, and we only knew that there is a holy God, and we had some familiarity with the history of our race. What conclusion would we

reach when we contemplate the problem of pleasure? One
does not need the Bible to know that we are a morally cul-
pable race, and that there is a holy God. When we ponder
the problem of pleasure, what would we think is the solution?

Is God Fattening Us For Slaughter?

It seems to me there are only two possibilities that
could very well occur to us. One is that God is fattening the
sheep for slaughter. That is, men are obviously wicked and
God is even more obviously holy. God must be angry with
us, and our troubled consciences confirm it. A moment's
reflection would tell us that we do not receive adequate
punishment in this world for our sins. Even though we are
hardened and calloused, and some of us have seared consciences, the generality of people know full well that we
have not been dealt with adequately by an infinitely holy
God, who we know must exist. We know that we are not
getting away with anything that He is not permitting us to
get away with. We know He is an infinitely powerful God,
who could take us in hand at any moment. We are equally
aware of the fact that He is not doing so. So we wonder, as
we tremble, whether He is simply allowing us to go on
until we are fat enough for His divine slaughter. It is an
awesome thought, to be sure, but an inevitable one when
we put one and one together: that is, the holiness of God
and the sinfulness of man.

We know there has to be a judgment coming. We also
know that our judgment will be according to our sins. We
recognize the gradations of sins among ourselves and in our
own law courts. We are aware that sin against God must be
infinitely more dreadful than any crime we commit against
one another. We try to fit our punishment to the crime, for
justice demands it, and we know that infinite justice must
do the same thing. We know that we are adding up sins
every day we live, which becomes less and less excusable
as we have more and more experience and knowledge about

God and the moral law. (If we are learning less and less, we are aware of the fact that that itself is a blameworthy thing.) We should be learning more and more, and that would make us more and more aware that we are becoming guiltier and guiltier. We obviously are built to learn from experience. If the more experience we have the less we learn, the more blameworthy we realize that we are.

We are infuriating the deity more and more. If He is a just and holy being, as we are led to believe, we are simply asking for it. Some criminals are so powerful that they can say to people whom they have marked out for death, "You're dead." They are not boasting; they have so much underworld power that they can liquidate most people they set their minds to remove. It is a dreadfully wicked power; but what power do they have except that which comes ultimately from the One who made them and sustains them, and without whose power they would not have any life, not to mention power, of their own?

There is no possibility of escaping God. Sometimes people get new identities and manage to escape the hitmen of the underworld. But who is ever going to escape God? Certainly not these criminals who have the audacity to say to innocent human beings, "You're dead." But not only they; they are just gross offenders. We are more sophisticated and refined ones. The more refined we are, the more aware we are that our sin can very well be more heinous than that of these crass professional criminals. No crime escapes the all-searching mind of the omniscient God.

The only reason we are getting away with it at the moment is that the Judge of heaven and earth has not seen fit to call us to account at this particular moment. We know we cannot escape. We know that we are only angering Him more and more with each passing day. We know that He, therefore, is permitting us to add sin to sin and become worthier and worthier of judgment, and so be certain recipients of an ever more terrible wrath.

We ask ourselves, "Is God letting us get away with it so

that, when our time is up, we will have accumulated enough sin to merit the wrath He has in store for us?" That is frightening, but no thoughtful person can deny its possibility. We see cattle grazing in the meadows and know that the farmer is feeding them for one ultimate purpose, namely to take them to market. Why are we sinners prospering?

Is God Waiting To Be Merciful?

The second thing that could occur to us as we ponder a God who is infinitely angry with us, yet not only withholding His infinite wrath, but actually showing us tokens of divine favor is this: He really loves us and wants us to turn away from our sins. If He passed final judgment now, we would have no such opportunity; that would be the end of time for us. He has sufficient provocation to do so; that we recognize. We have sinned enough to deserve His infinite wrath at any moment, but we do not receive it. We have an opportunity, therefore, to turn away from our sin and to turn to God. Instead of continuing to offend Him, we can plead for forgiveness and seek to please Him. While there is yet life, that is possible.

We are talking now as if there were no Bible, as if God had never revealed His purposes to us. As a mere guess, we could entertain the hope that God is sparing us now not to fatten us for the slaughter, but to save us from the slaughter.

Of course, He would have to be *merciful*. All He has to be to account for our judgment is holy and powerful. We know He is holy. We know He is powerful. To account for our being spared with the possibility of being saved from His wrath, He would have to be merciful.

Do we have any ground for hoping (other than the sheerest possibility) that He is a merciful God? There is nothing to stop us from hoping that He is. Since we know that we live on borrowed time and do not deserve a second more, we cannot help hoping that He may be sparing us in order to save us. We do not *know* that. We can prove from the existence of the world that He is all-powerful. We can prove from the way in which it is put together that He is all-wise. We can prove from our conscience that He is all-holy. What do we have to support the idea that He may also be merciful?

Mercy even with us is an optional virtue; we do not have to be merciful. We usually admire people who are, but we do not say that people must be so. We say everybody must be just. We say, for example, an employer, if he agrees to pay a certain wage, must pay that particular wage. If he does not pay it, then he is unjust and is liable to a lawsuit. All our contracts are based on the integrity and honesty and justice of people with whom we do business. They are actually subject to trials and imprisonment and even execution if they violate their duty of man to man. What about mercy among men? We love it. We admire it. We encourage it. We sometimes practice it. But we do not say mercy is obligatory.

Let us go back to that employer who must pay the worker what he has promised he would for an honest day's work. Does he have an obligation to give him a Christmas present? No. Does he have an obligation to pay his hospital bill? Not unless he has made it a part of his contract. Does he have an obligation to visit his employee when he is sick? No. That is not a part of any contract. Does he have to entertain his workers at his own home with his own family, or be friendly to them beyond his actual obligations? The answer is always "No." A worker may very well appreciate such actions when done by an employer, but he cannot demand them. He cannot fault the employer if he does not give them.

As a professor for thirty years, I had an obligation to teach my courses adequately, to grade students fairly, and to give them a proper basis for passing their examinations in accordance with their abilities. I could be faulted if I did not do those things, or even be reported to the president and the board, and ultimately fired if I failed to deliver on these obligations. Did I have an obligation to help a student outside of class? to give him extra hours? to spend time with him before examinations? and after the examinations to point out his mistakes and see if he could correct them so that the next time he would do better? No, none of those things was necessary. Some of us professors would do those things. No student could ever demand them. He had an obligation to be grateful for them if we gave them to him. On the other hand, our basic responsibilities were required, and a student could expect them, and we were reprehensible if we did not deliver. He did not have to thank us for them.

So we see, even in human affairs, that mercy is desirable. It is never, however, obligatory. We admire it when present. We do not censure for its absence.

If this is true even of human affairs, we can see immediately that God does not have to be merciful. He gave us life and conscience. He gave us intelligence to meet our obligations, and He has a right to hold us responsible for using them. He has no further obligation to forgive us if we do not. We say that the Judge of all the earth cannot do wrong, but we cannot say that the Judge of all the earth must be merciful.

As a matter of fact, and this is a frightening thought, there are grounds for thinking that God could not be merciful. If God were merciful, that would upset the balances of justice. If, as a professor, I had become compassionate with poor students and given them C's instead of F's, what an injustice that would be to the students who *earned* their C's. And students who earned F's would consider them of no significance. I would be an arbitrary professor who gave grades as I pleased. While I could not be just and give an A student a C, nevertheless I could be merciful and give a C student an A or an F student a C. The whole grading system would collapse. Good work and bad work would be indistinguishable.

Or, compare a judge who hears a case, but is allowed to exhibit mercy. He sees an individual who has committed a simple murder, but he feels compassionate toward him and sees fit to pardon him. He is a merciful judge and so that murderer goes free, but justice goes a-begging. We could never tolerate such behavior in a teacher, and certainly not in a judge. Our whole social fabric would be torn apart if mercy were allowed to make justice of no effect. Justice is obligatory; mercy is not. If mercy, which is optional, actually ruined justice, which is mandatory, mercy could not be permitted.

But thank God there is a place in human affairs where mercy may legitimately exist and not violate justice. If a judge, for example, after passing a proper and fair judgment on a criminal, does everything in his power to alleviate the suffering of the criminal's family and correct the behavior of that criminal, going far beyond the call of duty and doing something that is not necessary, that certainly would not harm justice. On the contrary, it would accentuate justice. This man would be an inflexibly righteous judge who never allowed mercy to cloud his judgment at the bench; but he would at the same time be a merciful person who, outside the courtroom and at a point where it never infringed on the justice of any of his sentences, went out of his way to be helpful to those whom justice condemned.

So we could begin to hope again. God could be merciful if He could be merciful in a way that did not violate His justice. His justice must be inflexible. Though God is merciful, He cannot throw the scales of justice out of balance.

How could God ever find a way that He could be merciful to us sinners and at the same time be just? Sins must be punished. How can we be punished and, at the same time, be the beneficiaries of divine mercy?

Take the analogy of the teacher and his student. The professor has first of all to be just, and the student flunks the course. He has to flunk the course; then the teacher can be merciful afterwards, going out of his way to help the student understand the course and prepare him so that, when he repeats the course, he will be able to meet the demands and pass it successfully, perhaps even well.

Apply that analogy to God. God has to punish us for our sins. That must be done, just as the F must be given by the professor. But an F by a professor is something which can be overcome. It is, after all, a temporal punishment, and it can be temporally corrected. Sins against God are of infinite enormity. When God punishes us for our sins, that means infinite wrath. If one goes under the unending wrath of God, how can mercy possibly help? The student with an F has a hope in this world. The person who goes into the next world under God's wrath has no hope.

This venture into speculative theology leaves us despairing, with a just God whose justice cannot be compromised. Therefore, He must punish us for our sins ultimately. That answers the problem of pleasure.

We have solved the problem of pleasure, a grim solution but a sound one. We are allowed to "enjoy" ourselves while the wrath of God remains over us only until He is ready to pour it out upon us. God is not mocked. Sinners are not really prospering. What is pleasure now turns out to be only a time of gathering an ever greater bundle of sticks for the sinner's own burning. "Whatever a man sows that shall he reap." The law of karma means an endless cycle of torments without any hope of nirvana. The Hindu religion senses this, but is afraid to say it. Most other religions sense it too, but try to whistle in the dark.

Where Mercy and Justice Meet

Only the Christian gospel resolves the problem of pleasure, and then offers a way that genuinely delivers us from it in a way in which justice and mercy kiss each other. Only Christ provides a true way of salvation from the dreadful predicament in which the problem of pleasure places man.

First, Christianity confirms the fact that justice must be satisfied. Sin must be condemned according to its demerit. This means eternal doom. The sinner must be damned because God must be inexorably holy and just. His all-powerful Being must vindicate His all-holy Being. Christianity never compromises the ever-blessed purity and excellency of the divine nature.

Second, Christianity alone finds a way to satisfy infinite justice and provide infinite mercy at the same time. What no other religion has dreamed of, Jesus Christ has accomplished. He underwent the infinite wrath of God against sin and lived to bestow His mercy on the damned sinners for whom He died. The infinite Son of God took upon Himself a human nature in which He underwent the full fury of the divine wrath. The omnipotent God satisfied His violated holiness by punishing sin completely in His blessed Son, who "became sin" for His people. The justice of God was vindicated in full in the substitute, His own Son, our Savior dear. He survived that awful vengeance and rose victor over the grave by the power of His own divinity. Now He offers to every sin-sick and "pleasure"-burdened soul an everlasting mercy. Perfect mercy and perfect justice in the gospel of the crucified One are here and now offered to you, dear reader.

Now the problem of pleasure has its answer in full. God has spared you, not that you be damned, but that you be saved from the damnation that otherwise would inevitably have been your destiny. Now Jesus Christ stands at the door of your heart and offers to come in and dwell with you forevermore: "Come unto Me, all ye who are weary and heavy-laden, and I will give you rest."

Real Pleasure Forever

You who are burdened with your "pleasures" now have the opportunity to escape. Continue as you are and every moment you go on will be "pleasure" more or less ("hell"

on earth is "heaven" for the lost); but that "pleasure" you
do not deserve will only add to the everlasting condemnation you do deserve if you do not turn to Jesus
Christ. Your present "pleasure" is your opportunity for
real pleasure in the presence of a reconciled God, your
Father. Spurn the offer of real pleasure and you will be
damned by your spurious pleasure. Receive the offer of joy
forevermore and you will realize the purpose for which you
have your "pleasures" to this very moment: that you
should be given this opportunity now to have *true pleasure
forevermore*—

"At Thy right hand there are pleasures for evermore"
(Psalm 16:11).